THE Forgotten Fairies

Find out more about M.T. Lott at:
mtlottbooks.com
www.facebook.com/authormtlott

ISBN: 978-1-7337468-0-9

BOOKS BY M.T. LOTT

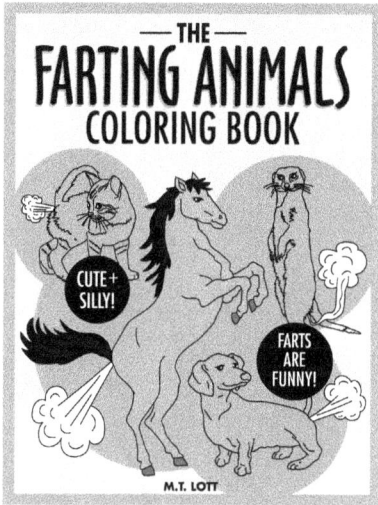

THE FARTING ANIMALS COLORING BOOK
CUTE + SILLY!
FARTS ARE FUNNY!
M.T. LOTT

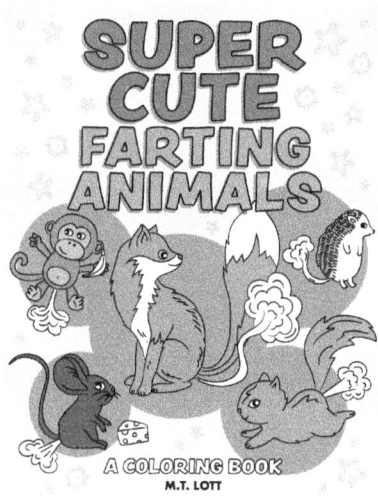

SUPER CUTE FARTING ANIMALS
A COLORING BOOK
M.T. LOTT

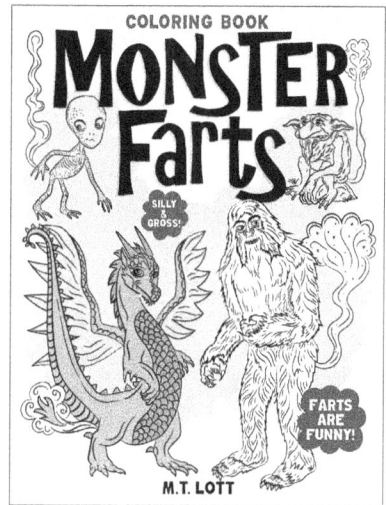

COLORING BOOK
MONSTER Farts
SILLY & GROSS!
FARTS ARE FUNNY!
M.T. LOTT

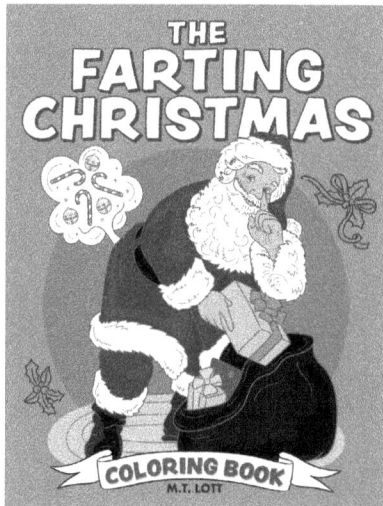

THE FARTING CHRISTMAS
COLORING BOOK
M.T. LOTT

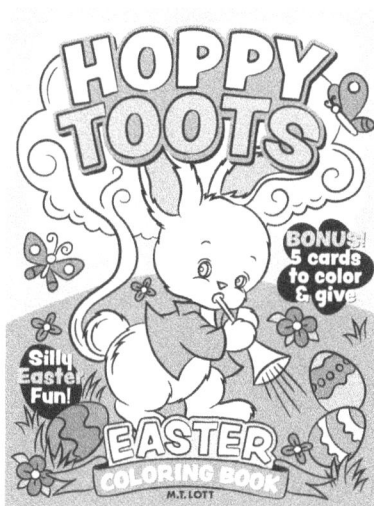

HOPPY TOOTS
BONUS! 5 cards to color & give
Silly Easter Fun!
EASTER COLORING BOOK
M.T. LOTT

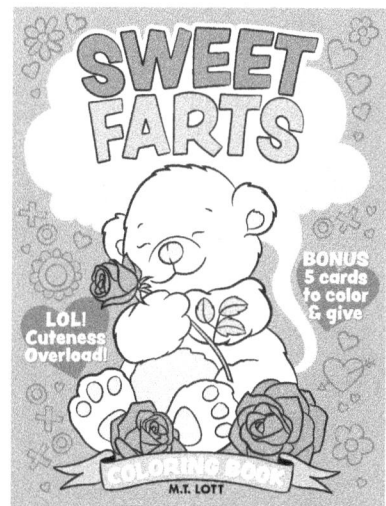

SWEET FARTS
BONUS 5 cards to color & give
LOL! Cuteness Overload!
COLORING BOOK
M.T. LOTT

Forgotten Fairies: Book One
Annabelle
The Reluctant Fart Fairy
BY M.T. LOTT

Forgotten Fairies: Book Two
Annabelle
And The Fairy Hunter
BY M.T. LOTT

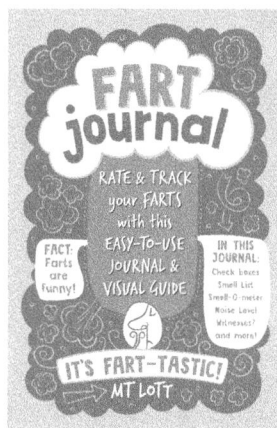

FART journal
RATE & TRACK your FARTS with this EASY-TO-USE JOURNAL & VISUAL GUIDE
FACT: Farts are funny!
IN THIS JOURNAL: Check boxes, Smell List, Smell-O-meter, Noise Level, Witnesses? and more!
IT'S FART-TASTIC!
MT LOTT

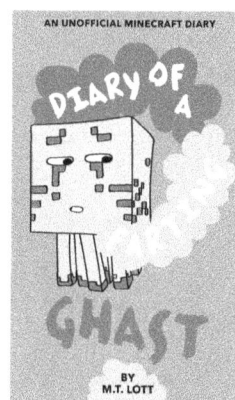

AN UNOFFICIAL MINECRAFT DIARY
DIARY OF A FARTING GHAST
BY M.T. LOTT

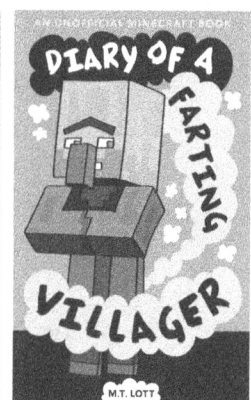

AN UNOFFICIAL MINECRAFT BOOK
DIARY OF A FARTING VILLAGER
M.T. LOTT

Slug Fairy

She knows happy and healthy slugs leave
the best slime trails in the forest.

Crab Grass Fairy

This fairy happily makes crab grass appear
in the most carefully cultivated lawn.

Rat Fairy

She sees the goodness in the heart of every rat.

Algae Fairy

She can make any pond or
lake slimy and green.

Fly Fairy

She makes sure they have all the
love and attention they need.

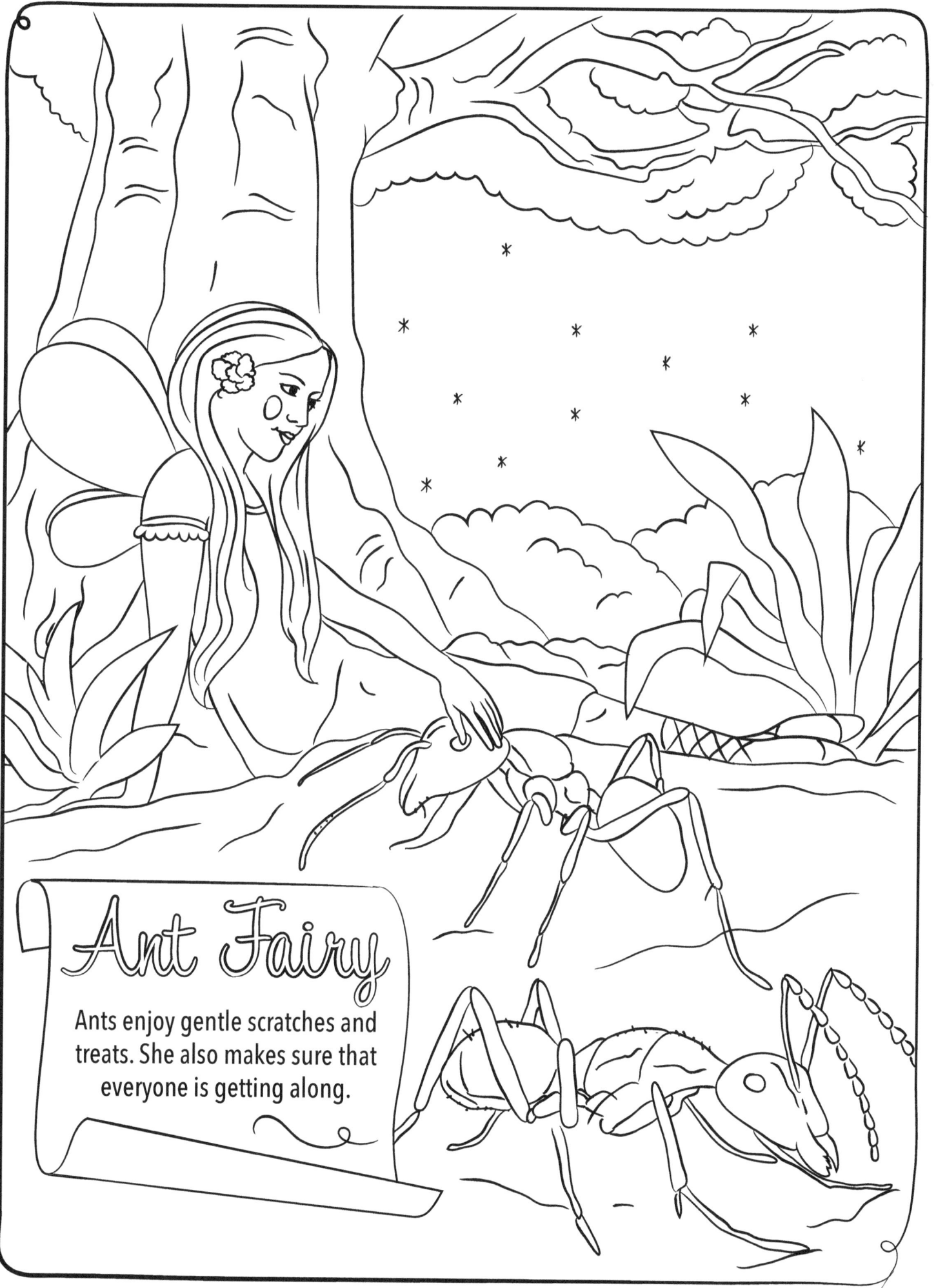

Ant Fairy

Ants enjoy gentle scratches and treats. She also makes sure that everyone is getting along.

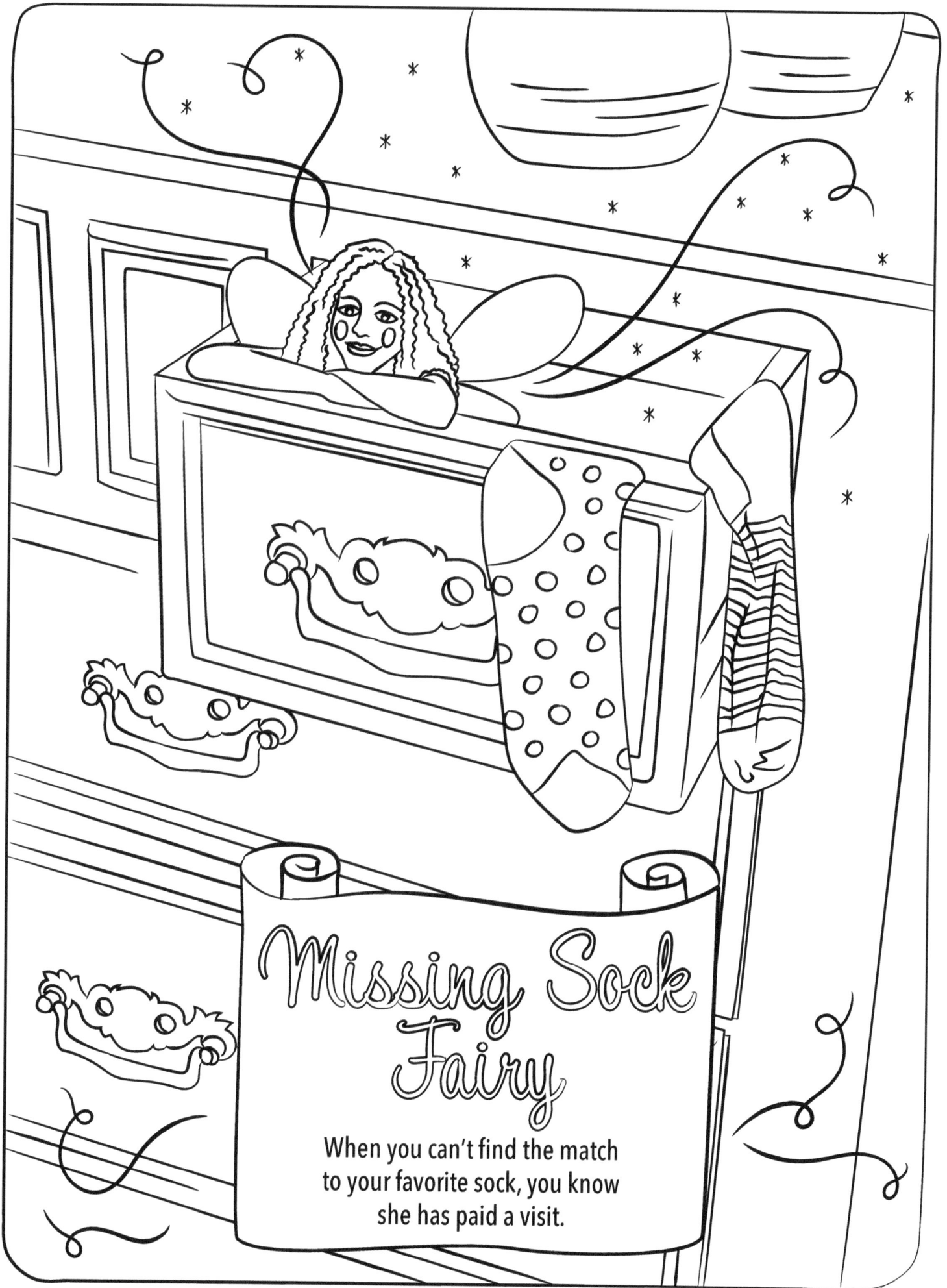

Missing Sock Fairy

When you can't find the match
to your favorite sock, you know
she has paid a visit.

Lost Glove Fairy

Her magic makes it fall right out of your pocket.

Dust Bunny Fairy

A most creative fairy, who sculpts dust into familiar shapes.

Clogged Sink Fairy

A very mischevious fairy. She enjoys seeing people struggle with a plunger.

Litter Box Fairy

Cats do most of the work but she makes sure it's extra stinky.

Brown Banana Fairy

She'll turn your yellow bananas brown in the blink of an eye.

Fart Fairy

It's true, we all pass gas and a fairy makes it happen.

Bed Head Fairy

You always know when she's visited.

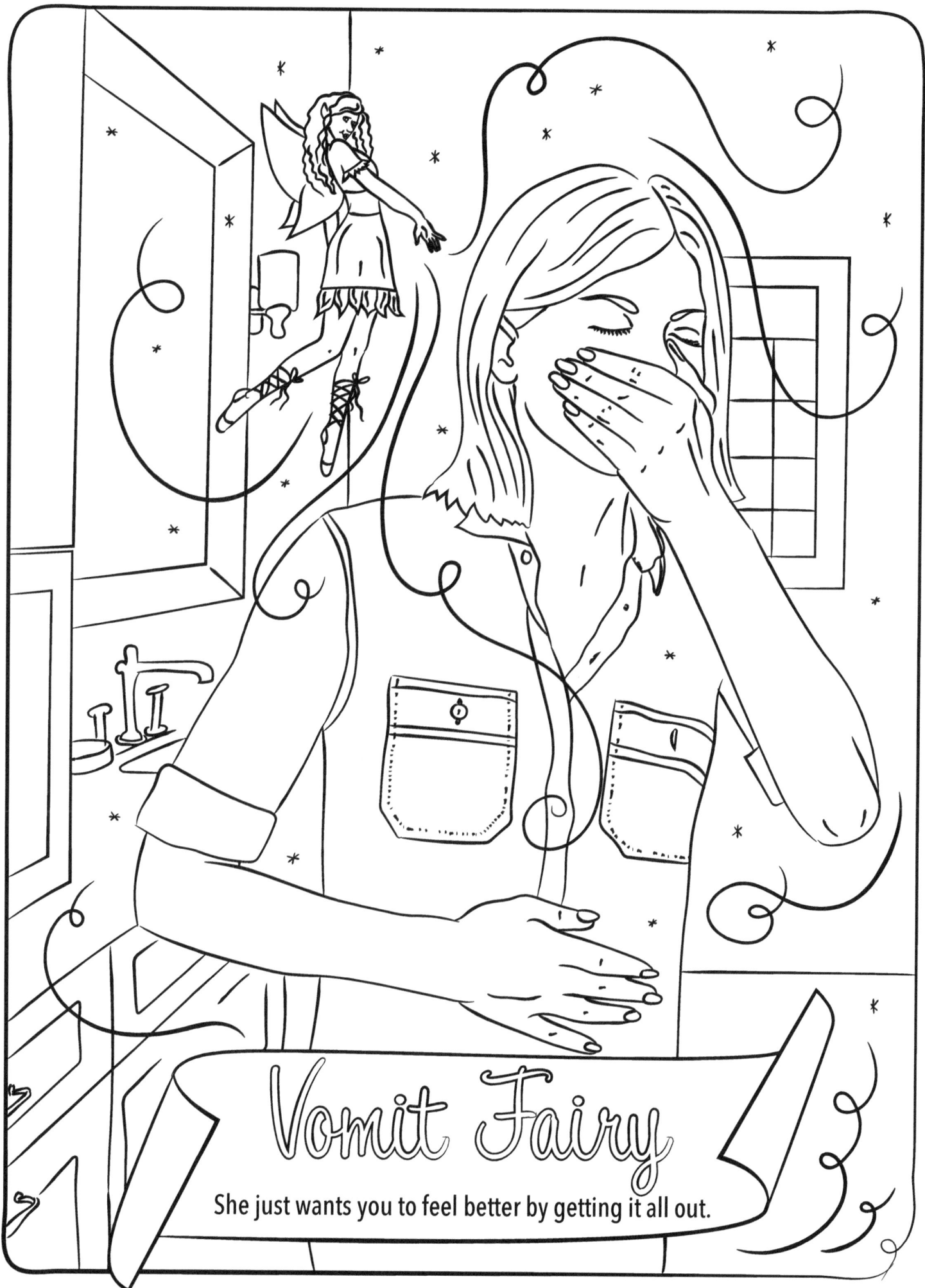

Vomit Fairy

She just wants you to feel better by getting it all out.

Body Odor Fairy

When you're really stinky, you know she's paid a visit.

Stuck Zipper Fairy

She's an expert in making it impossible to budge!

Sunburn Fairy

Ouch! She knows when you forgot the sunscreen.

Stinky Dog Fairy

Dogs actually enjoy when she visits!

Hairball

She knows your poor kitty was cleaning herself a little too much.

www.ingramcontent.com/pod-product-compliance
Lightning Source LLC
Chambersburg PA
CBHW080632030426

42336CB00018B/3161